The Needs of Living Things

Ruby Lee

Series Editor
Kathleen Corrigan

Animals and plants are living things.

Animals and plants have needs.

Animals need water and air.
They need sunlight too.

Animals need food.
They need a home too.

That's Amazing!

Plants use the sun to make food.

Plants need water and air.
They also need sunlight.

Plants need a home.

You are a living thing.
What do you need?

Plants need a home.

